STANDING IN LINE FOR THE BEAST

New Issues Poetry & Prose

Managing Editor   Marianne Swierenga

Copy Editor   Elizabeth Marzoni

Assistant to the Editor Kimberly Kolbe

New Issues Poetry & Prose
The College of Arts and Sciences
Western Michigan University
Kalamazoo, MI 49008

An Inland Seas Poetry Book

 Inland Seas poetry books are supported by a grant from
The Michigan Council for Arts and Cultural Affairs.

First Edition, 2007.

ISBN-10   1-930974-67-1 (paperbound)
ISBN-13   978-1-930974-67-8 (paperbound)

Library of Congress Cataloging-in-Publication Data:
Bredle, Jason
Standing in line for the beast/Jason Bredle
Library of Congress Control Number: 2006937309

Art Director   Tricia Hennessy
Designer   Lindsay Steele
Production Manager   Paul Sizer
                     The Design Center, School of Art
                     College of Fine Arts
                     Western Michigan University

STANDING IN LINE FOR THE BEAST

JASON BREDLE

New Issues

 WESTERN MICHIGAN UNIVERSITY

for my parents

Contents

Jason Bredle's Technicolor World of Beasts and Lovers

What do meatballs, Korean soap operas, Dorothy Wordsworth's journals, a joke about women's tennis, underpants, minivans, and Mexico have in common? Maybe nothing or maybe everything, but they're all crammed into "When Disaster Stikes 4," a wonderful poem in Jason Bredle's exhilarating book *Standing in Line for the Beast*. And what a beast it is. These long loopy poems make you laugh out loud and then crumple your heart like a Dixie cup. They are like riding a roller coaster at the fun park after eating too many foot longs, but you've never been happier.

The first thing I found myself loving about these poems was that they would consider anything. They do not come from a rarified pseudo-European Poetry World constructed by Rilke and Paul Celan wannabes, a breathless world where people are just too sensitive or confused or mired in their childhoods for words. The world of a Bredle poem is a world in which people watch television, go to parties, get drunk, have their hearts broken, tell jokes, read books, shop for chocolate milk, eat enchiladas. And a lot of them take place in the Midwest, which has never seemed so luminous or so strange. Who knew that Cincinnati, Terre Haute, Nebraska could be so ordinary and other worldly at the same time? And these are not skimpy poems but full-bodied Jayne Mansfield poems careening with images, jokes, and words, words, words. This is a poet who is taking advantage of the English language, and not the English of a hundred years ago but the English that is exploding from our streets, TVs, newspapers, and radios.

It is difficult to enumerate the pleasures of this book—the wacky adventures, the Polaroids of our fast food life, the car trips, the beer parties, the miniature golf and bowling—but let me try. First, there is the poem that begins "The horse discovered a gateway to another / dimension" and then proceeds to move around the universe: through the French Revolution, into Franco's living room, on to The Price is Right and the Senate floor, ending up in a place so lovely that the bite and irony of the preceding lines disappear like fireworks in the night sky. Or there's "Girls, Look Out for

Todd Bernstein," which among other things contains a hilarious digression about a television sitcom that features a TV repairperson who finds herself in the "living room of a family / of barbarian warlords on a planet near / Alpha Centauri." One of my favorite poems is "Summer," which begins:

> If you ever eat too many enchiladas
> don't go over to your ex-girlfriend's
> apartment immediately afterwards, rip off
> your pants and have sex with her, because
> unbelievable cramps will be the least
> of your problems.

What comes next is a list of problems both magical and mundane, like a snapshot of the mind of the friend you've always wanted or wanted to be. Jason Bredle loves a list, and "Summer" contains lists inside of lists, ending with Mr. Scrambles and an image so modern and ancient that Homer might have written it if he'd known what a telephone answering machine was.

These poems attack basic human desires, such as wanting to turn into a werewolf so you can tear the throat out of a crashing bore. Or picturing Hell or characterizing death, which in a Jason Bredle poem can take you from listening to his friend Anne read a poem to a thunderstorm in Memphis to Mexico to "an 18 / wheeler hauling Little Debbie snack cakes up I-75" and beyond. Jason Bredle is in that truck, eating Little Debbie cakes and being kicked in the ass by Kierkegaard, heading to Mexico to fall in love or die, because either one could be just around the corner.

—Barbara Hamby

Acknowledgments

Thanks to the editors of the following journals, where versions of some of these poems first appeared:

The Cream City Review, "Frida Kahlo"; *Green Mountains Review*, "The Horse's Adventure," "Girls, Look Out for Todd Bernstein," "No Story, Just a Comment on Some of Anne's Poems," "While Anne Reads a Lengthy Poem about Her Grandmother's Funeral and Our Mortality"; *Indiana Review*, "Marc McKee"; *Mississippi Review*, "Anarchy"; *Missouri Review*, "The Right Hand of Karma Is Extending Its Middle Finger," "Readings," "Other Readings,"; *New Hampshire Review*, "Intramural Correspondence"; *Phoebe*, "Werewolves"; *Salt Hill*, "The Classic Story," "Desperation," "Parasol"; *Spoon River Poetry Review*, "Hell"; *TriQuarterly*, "Apocalypse," "The Year of Living Regrettably,"; *20 Pounds of Headlights*, "Summer."

"Girls, Look Out for Todd Bernstein" also appeared in *180 More: Extraordinary Poems for Every Day* (Random House, 2005).

Some of these poems were inspired by the following: Gastr del Sol's "Blues Subtitled No Sense of Wonder," Bill Viola: A 25 Year Survey, October 16, 1999 to January 9, 2000 at the Art Institute of Chicago, Mike Kelley's *Confusion: A Play in Seven Sets, Each Set More Spectacular and Elaborate Than the Last*, John Ashbery's *April Galleons*, Michael Ondaatje, Rick Moody, Ralph Burns, Tim O'Brien, ESPN, Dorothy Wordsworth.

A version of this manuscript was granted a prize in the Avery Hopwood and Jule Hopwood Contest for 2000 at the University of Michigan.

Thank you to my family and friends for your continued love and support throughout the years.

Visit the author's website: www.knifemachine.com

Once I was passing a roadside fruit stand, and I stopped to ask for directions. There was an old grizzled farmer there, with a face that looked like he had seen many things in his life. I asked him which way to go. He paused for a moment, then took out a handkerchief and wiped his brow. I don't know what he said, because I just peeled out. I don't have time for guys to pull out handkerchiefs.

—Jack Handey

But the rushing—tell me it's going somewhere.

—Marc McKee

On the Way to the 53-B District Court of Livingston County, October 1, 1999

It begins while eating something extremely
erotic, like a cake with a picture of two
people making out on it. It begins on a Friday
night, driving to Lansing with Anne. It begins
before that, with the line, He was interested
in this turn of events. It begins with
$148.77 worth of phone calls
to Ypsilanti. It begins at the possibility
of sailing the ocean blue, with all its oceany
blueness. It begins when you never go sailing
off the coast of North Carolina,
when your father leaves a package on an empty
boat in Norfolk, Virginia. It begins
when your best friend sends you a letter
about walking to Bigfoot to buy NyQuil
for his asshole friend Nick, about
meeting a woman there who lives across
the street, a woman who wants to read Tarot
for him. It begins when she draws the death card.
Typically, you hate your name, but for some
reason, right at that moment, when he's written,
At least I'd have a funny story for Jason,
your name seems beautiful to you. It begins with
the two of you in Taco Bell on a Tuesday
night. No, it begins in a Chinese
take-out place that same night.
Or maybe it begins on the corner of Third
and Woodlawn, where you're standing alone,
a breeze blowing your hair to the right, the traffic
rushing leftward, where Richard has envisioned
his own death. It begins with a message
on someone's machine at three AM,
a message saying, That's it, in the past
hour I've found myself naked in someone

else's bed and had my driver's license
confiscated. It begins when that message is lost.
It begins as you stand alone and confused
in the setting sun at a pay phone in Cougar,
Washington. It begins with a story about holidays,
a story that really isn't about holidays
but instead how it feels to want so badly
to love your family and not be able to, to want
to live a normal life but to know it's impossible.
It begins when you read this story, or really,
afterwards, as you're sitting by yourself
in Tubby's next to the Dog Wall of Fame,
watching everyone with somewhere to be go by.
It begins on a Monday night as you're waiting
for her to call. It begins when she doesn't,
or rather, the following day when you're writing
something about Tubby's and your neighbor's just
rowed out on the lake and the sky's turned
pinkish and cold and she calls, and to hear
her voice today of all days
and to talk about gymnastics which you may
or may not like and the person she's loved
ever since she left you for him,
about you having your license confiscated,
to do these things, you feel, means something—
like being handed pamphlets about Jesus.
No, no. Scratch all that. It begins
when a gray cat walks into your house and falls
asleep on a green jacket. It begins as you're falling
asleep on the coast of Maine, the lights of Portland
eight miles away in the distance. It begins
on Mount St. Helen's when Kirk pees
into the lava dome. It begins later that evening
as you're taking the red eye from Seattle to Detroit
and you're so thirsty not even all

the Pepsi in the world will keep you from drinking
the lavatory bathwater. Wait, no,
it begins the last time you're holding the woman
you love outside her door in central Mexico,
August 2, 1997. It begins
earlier than that, in a hotel room in Pátzcuaro
on the Fourth of July, in bed with her, never
wanting to fall asleep, never wanting
that moment to end. And back home
someone you don't know yet is falling
in love with his Shakespeare professor and a year
later you'll be watching your second cousins
shoot off bottle rockets in Plainfield,
Indiana, during the longest fireworks
display you'll ever see. Your grandmother's there.
And now you wonder if you'll ever see her
again. It's been since April, and you called her once,
but it's not the same as it used to be, it's not
like playing bingo in her living room,
the only game she ever had, feeling
someone's unconditional love, one
that today you fear you may never feel again.
And the rest of the time you're just trying to find that,
and knowing that it may never happen again
is unbearable. It begins with an old photo,
the colors pale, worn out. It's cold outside.
You're wearing a red and blue coat, a hat.
Somebody had to take that picture, somebody
had to. It begins with a letter from your best friend
and the death card. It begins with a woman saying
someone you have just come to know or will come
to know very well soon will be a mess
on the inside and will keep you from what
you're supposed to do. It begins with a phone call
to Anne, a long distance call to Ypsilanti.

It begins when you don't feel like you can take it
anymore, in someone's living room
where you're forced to name your favorite state
in the union, a room that seems to be lit
by candles but which isn't. It begins when
somebody cuts you in the buffet line at a local
restaurant. This tastes like homemade strawberry
pie, are you sure it isn't? It begins with someone
telling you to take care of your face, a phone
being ripped from a wall, a shotgun
fired indoors on a Thursday morning, the memory
of a Nova Scotia sunset last winter.
It begins one morning when you receive
a phone call and no one speaks on the other
end. It begins when you hang up
and glance out the window toward the lake. It begins
when you see over a dozen swans swimming
toward you, and it never ends.

Anarchy

In a world where kids call bad pizzas
circles of death and spend their Saturday
afternoons engaged in games of earthball
so violently competitive one could safely
label them quasi-erotic, you better
believe you'll see some hot-shot
teenager gallivanting around town in shorts
during what local television newscasts
will have christened Winter Blast Xtreme just
as you should expect to see a group of drunken
townspeople riding in the back of a pickup
through the Wal-Mart parking lot
waving a Confederate flag as if there were no
tomorrow and Anarchy had just leapt into
that blue Trans Am and sped off
to the state capital for some good old-fashioned
drinking and womanizing. Things will have
come to that, and this time you can expect
to see Anarchy achieve some freaking results.
I mean, in the past he's made some poor
decisions that've postponed world
domination and the grand rise of mass
turmoil (i.e. propositioning
a woman sexually who it turned out
was a freaking cop, breaking both his legs
while trying to jump five luxury vans
on his motorcycle, spooking the hell
out of some cattle one night who he later
decided must've been in cahoots with the freaking
cops), but he's learned from them and guaranteed
not to foul anything up again.
So look out world because Charles Atlas
isn't going to step in, take off
his shirt, and flex for a while to make everything

better this time—Anarchy will chew him up
like a bucket of gizzards because muscle mass
doesn't impress him. He was in downtown
Louisville last Halloween rounding up a posse
for Belligerence Expo, a four-week seminar
instilling not only the values of basic
rowdiness but also full-blown, face-slapping
chaos into its attendees—a program he began
working on in the ninth grade while bouncing
around his room in his underpants
eating Corn Flakes, watching soft-core porn
on Cinemax, decorating his jean jacket
with cool Metallica and AC/DC patches,
screening and re-screening *Triumph of the Will*,
reading books about the Night Stalker
and Mussolini, and giving himself tattoos
by way of a rusty needle, frayed wire,
two C batteries, and a jar of green
ink (tattoos proclaiming his adoration for,
among other things, anarchy, Metallica,
AC/DC, the devil and all things demonic,
crucifixes, etc.). And eventually his scheme burst
forth from a swimming pool like an emotionally
unstable pony gasping for breath: total world
domination. So now he's on his way,
crawling out of Tailgators rejuvenated

and swarming with energy, ready to crash the tea
party at any moment, overturn
tables, bash some finger sandwich trays
against the wall, and toss scalding hot tea
onto the crotches of the most distinguished
individuals, ready to bust in yowling
during Noam Chomsky's acceptance speech
at the Player of the Year Awards and jam

the statuette down Chomsky's throat. I mean,
you never know when it'll all go down—
you could be driving down the street
in your Mazda minding your own business
when all of a sudden this bearded lunatic leaps
onto the hood of your car and bashes your windshield
with a brick in a fit of lumberjackial rage; you
could be in your living room reading up on what
kids these days are calling bad pizzas
in your teen slang book when through the window
leaps this madman named Anarchy who starts
smashing all your knickknacks and mantelpieces
with an aluminum bat; you could be at 7-11
on Christmas Eve when a Ford Escort comes
barreling through the front door and out steps
a drunk woman who breaks every cheap
wine bottle in sight and then in pops
Anarchy with a tire iron and a score to settle
with the night manager; you could be at Ponderosa
on the verge of biting into some meat gone wildly
bad when you're distracted by this barbarianesque
wildman overturning the sundae bar
and breaking tables over the heads of senior citizens;
you could be down at the club working
on your electrifying backhand when in parachutes
this manimal in a jumpsuit who lands on your back
and begins gnawing at your neck; you could be
playing Trivial Pursuit with your ex-girlfriend,
trying to answer a question about which sport
uses the biggest ball when out of the closet
bursts Anarchy, breaking the board over your head
while crying out in the same extraterrestrial
war chant we'll someday hear that moment
we're all anally probed and zapped through time

and space to serve as slaves for a civilization
of Bytrons on some three-sunned planet
in M31; you could be in Cheyenne,
in Santa Clara del Cobre having not showered
in days, in Miami, on your way to Asheville
with someone you love but it won't matter, he'll take
her away regardless, and henceforward you'll keep
that empty Tropicana bottle and razor
blade on your dresser and I'll always carry
140 pesos with me wherever I go.

Subtitled

Attention: last week I witnessed two
people being condemned to Hell, subtitled
Where does one find the ability to deal
with things rationally? For instance, three days
ago I was stuck in traffic for two and a half
hours on I-94 behind both a wiener
truck and a couple in an Oldsmobile who
wouldn't stop making out, subtitled
Crossing a state line, subtitled A room
with a spinning mirror. The one who sees.
A figure in black amongst a field of marigolds.
Subtitled I'm sorry I don't love her, subtitled
The first was a meter maid who was told
she was an evil woman who would burn in Hell.
Subtitled We all make mistakes, and some
ruin it for everyone, subtitled North Judson:
A Town with a Future. Part of me will always
be driving Sarah back from Evansville. Subtitled
How do people deal with things, as in
shopping at Meijer? How does one find
the extension cords, or someone who knows
the location of the extension cords? It's like riding
an escalator toward a tiny room on top
of a mountain. Inside, marigolds, yes, candles
and rosary beads. Subtitled Trying to deal
with it all, that is, subtitled You just want to eat
your elbow while standing in the checkout
for over half an hour with your extension cord
and the Christmas music and the one hundred top
entertainers of all time and all
of a sudden you need to use a lot of exclamation
points! Like right here! For example!
Then one night you have a dream

you're wearing this gigantic turtleneck sweater
and you think, Damn, this looks surprisingly
fantastic on me, subtitled That same
night Kirk dreams that you've died, subtitled
The other was me, who was condemned to Hell
by a random caller to a local radio show.
Subtitled Where do you go at this point?
Subtitled You can see the tiny room
from Calle Sangre de Cristo. Sometimes you just
can't go on. It's impossible. Isn't it? Subtitled
In the geographic center of the country stands
an eighty-ton statue of Jesus. Subtitled
Screaming, subtitled A honeydew melon,
subtitled The train's coming, brace yourself
for the disaster. Subtitled Your father falls thirteen
feet, your mother hides boxes of wine
under the sink. Subtitled Then one night,
she wanders home with a busted lip and you drive
to the observatory and it's so cold, it's winter
and there's nothing to do but go up
to the observatory or some other such place,
say the river, say, the cliff overlooking
the river or just drive around aimlessly
all the way to Kentucky and overcome your fear
of heights on a water tower along the way.
Subtitled An owl on three walls, a man
sleeping. Subtitled The one who sees. A girl
is patting a horse for seven hours, a man
is firing a shotgun skyward in the middle of a city.
Subtitled Say your grace, eat your vegetables
and don't complain. I was there last week,
where were you, Sarah? Where were you?
Subtitled How do people deal with things?

As in the question mark, as in road rage?
Oh, I'm the guy in the SUV
who never learned that the left lane is for passing
and the right lane is for douchebags like me.
Or, say, stop lights. Subtitled
A lamp in an aquarium, a plastic deer on a stage.
Ladies and gentlemen, please put your hands
together and give a warm welcome for
THE DEER! Subtitled The vase of insects
has been knocked over, a champagne glass broken
on the steps of the banquet hall. Subtitled Watching
you is like watching spiders grow
into beautiful pillows, subtitled It's a room
with a spinning mirror. Things are said, but they're
of no importance at this point, subtitled
And then you're four years old and your father's
taking you to Southside Liquor, subtitled
The bourbon's in cases behind the furnace,
subtitled You grow up, subtitled How
do people deal with things in a rational manner?
Subtitled This is the story of a boy spiraling
into the arms of women who don't love him,
subtitled And then what are you supposed to do,
forget about what it feels like to touch
someone's hand on a bus to Mexico City?
Forget about the feeling of her fingers brushing
across the back of your neck? Subtitled
There are moments where everything is perfect,
moments, under a table with a plate of carrot
sticks, for example, subtitled Will I ever stop
loving you, and if so, when will it end?
Subtitled Father's gone away for a few
months, but he'll be back soon, and you

can visit him every other weekend,
besides. Subtitled How is it people deal
with things, again? Last night, at 1:30,
the man across the street was burning an immense
pile of things, drunk, listening to the Minutemen,
and then this morning a pumpkin washed up
on the lakeshore. It's like when you leave
your mother and everything's fine, but you forget,
say, a glass fish, return home
and find her there, in the breakfast nook,
crying.

Parasol

Jesus Christ, Suzanne hung that parasol
in the corner of the room and now all
our thoughts and conversations either make
direct references to parasols or can somehow
be linked to the parasol. You know, how we sit
cowering below the parasol on this tiny,
backless couch, the clock ticking like a parasol
tapping another parasol, the three o'clock
parasol parasoling a wistful parasol.
And when you refer to the man waving
his rubber thumb I'll know you meant to say
parasol and when you ask if I want
to eat a rattlesnake I'll be thinking, parasol?
And the parasol will become an object of loathing
and I'll begin my personal vendetta against
the parasol, and I swear to you, friend,
that I will eat, sleep, and breathe the extermination
of that parasol until the morning comes when you
and Suzanne leave and I break in
and have my way with it. It won't be pretty.
I'll break it over Julie Piepmeyer's
head, repeatedly, take a saw to it, let
the dog bite it, burn it, and I'll hurl those ashes
into the Ohio River like I did my guitar after weeks
of practicing and not obtaining rock stardom
or the female companionship associated with rock
stardom. And then you'll see me smiling
like a parasol covering Tom Wopat at the Fall
Festival parade and a horse will look at you
from a beach before the setting sun as if
to ask, Why is this dining room chair
sitting here, and the beauty of it will be
it'll have nothing to do with parasols. And I'll
storm into your house like some flagrant

parasol to eat a salad like a dainty
parasol and a piece of chicken that goes down
about as well as a parasol and you'll be
wondering, Whatever happened to the parasol
and I'll act dumbfounded like the president's
parasol when asked about his illicit affairs
and everything will return to normal, except there
will be no more parasol talk. Then Suzanne
will put out this wicker wastebasket
with all these aggressive plants protruding
from the lid that'll become so distracting I'll begin
placing corn cobs in my pockets to avoid
thinking about the wastebasket.

Girls, Look Out for Todd Bernstein

Because after sitting out for a spell
he's back with a degree in accounting and a high
paying position in one of the leading
pharmaceutical corporations in the country
and aspirations of owning that exotic yellow
sports car, license plate EVIL.
And like Dennis Meng at Sycamore Chevrolet
stakes his reputation on his fully reconditioned
used cars, I stake my reputation
on telling you Todd Bernstein means business
this time, girls. No more of this being passed over
for abusive arm wrestling stars. He's got
a velour shirt now. No more of your excuses—
if he wants you, you're there. None of this
I'm shaving my pubes Friday night nonsense—
come on, you think Todd Bernstein's
going to fall for that? He knows you're not
studying, not busy working on some local
political campaign, not having the guy
who played Cockroach on *The Cosby Show* over
for dinner, not writing any great American
novel. He's seen your stuff and it's nothing more
than mediocre lyric poetry with titles
like "The Falling" and "Crucible" and "Waking to Death"
that force impossible metaphors, despairing
about love and womanhood and how bad
your life is even though you grew up happily
in suburban America, or at least as happily
as anyone can grow up in suburban America,
which normally, you know, consists of
the appearance of happiness while your dad is doing
three secretaries on the side and your mom
pretends not to know and brags to the entire

town about how you're an actress about to star
in a sitcom about the misadventures of a cable TV
repairperson who, while out on a routine
installation one day, accidentally
electrically blasts herself into the living room
of a family of barbarian warlords on a planet
near Alpha Centauri who force her into slavery
before sending her on a pillage mission
to a planet of Cloxnors who capture her and place
her in a torture institution where she meets
a vulnerable Meeb whom she convinces, because of
her cable TV repairperson skills, to let her
become nanny to its impressionable Meeblets just
before it's about to rip off her limbs
with its ferocious abnons and devour her.
The results, according to your mom, are hilarious,
but come on, you and I both know the story
is just so *predictable*. And Todd knows
your writing doesn't pull off any metaphors
for the happiness taken from you by some dude
who played bass and called himself a musician
when all he could really do was play a couple
of chords and sing about true love and alligators
and how the alligator represents true love
which somehow explains the legend where the guy
cut open an alligator one time in Florida
and found a golfer. There's just no fooling
Todd. Sure, he'll act like he's interested, that's
Todd Bernstein, and he'll make claims
that he too has written or been artistic
at some point in his life, but Todd Bernstein
knows all you girls really want is a piece
of good old Todd Bernstein. No longer

will any strange auras enter the bedroom
during sex and keep him from maintaining
an erection, no longer will any women
walk out on him repulsed. If anybody's walking out
after sex, it'll be Todd Bernstein, I can assure you.
He won't be humiliating himself by falling down
a flight of stairs in front of a group of Japanese
tourists anymore, but rather coaxing entire
masses of women into his bedroom. Because
that's Todd Bernstein. He's on the move.
And he wants you to know, girls, that he's well aware
you certainly can't learn Korean sitting around here
which is why he's out there right now, preparing
for the slew of women just beyond his sexual
horizon, spray-painting GIRLS, LOOK OUT
FOR TODD BERNSTEIN on the side
of a Village Pantry.

The Classic Story

Imagine: it's not one of those summer evenings
when a cold front is dropping down
from the north and colliding with a mass
of face-slapping humidity, exploding into this
tornado-dropping thunderstorm resembling
a dance party gone punch-spillingly,
leg-breakingly wrong, where one second
you're engorged by the latest marketed craze,
dancing like you've just discovered your hands
for the first time, and the next the Lord
of the Underworld is sprouting up beside a guy
wearing one of those tuxedo shirts, warbling
everyone into an orgiastic banquet of break dancing
violence—but instead, one of those days
you're crouching behind a birdbath on Linda's
front lawn trying to figure out a way
to conspicuously deliver this grapefruit with a knife
through it to her doorstep and I'm up here
cutting photos out of *Cosmopolitan*
and *Gun Dog Magazine*, pasting them in creative
collages on orange construction paper and mailing
them to my ex-girlfriend. But what can I say,
these are the days of our post-whimsical,
neo-absurdist lives, in which our goal
has become surviving each hour without
breaking down publicly—because it's hard
to believe we could be post/neo-anything
in such a technologically advanced era,
but it sure feels like it when our only escape
from the mercilessness of "reality" involves
ludicrous fantasies that include rewiring
our enemies' (so many at this point, it's hard
to believe!) cars for explosion while wearing purple

capes and leopard print, g-string underpants—
I guess, though, if that were to happen we could
at least think we'd achieved something, couldn't we?
And who knows, maybe these fantasías
would open doors or something and we'd have more
of a future than some cold, unforgiving
field in the middle of Kansas and one day
we'd be in all the history books as those
who created the venganza dulce market, thereby
ridding the world of all wrongdoers. Anyway!
I'm here, to say the least, jammed in the middle
of the classic story: boy meets girl,
boy and girl fall in love after becoming
chemistry lab partners, girl inflates
used condom till it explodes in boy's face,
girl's father blows hole in wall in attempt
to kill girl's mother, girl leaves boy
at prom, boy meets girl through another girl
obsessed with Charles Manson, boy and girl
fall in love, girl wins lawsuit after car
accident leaves her permanently scarred, boy
moves to New Jersey, boy moves back,
boy has affair with different girl in middle
of Mexico, previous girl leaves boy
upon his return and discovery that she'd been
cheating on him for over a year, fiancé
of girl with whom boy had affair in Mexico begins
harassing boy, calling him while drunk
late at night, boy meets girl,
girl weaves a series of lies so complex
boy can't even begin to explain—boy
wins upstart cable television network
dance contest, boy marries girl

from that ionized bracelet commercial, midwestern
winter sky proves impenetrable, Heaven
remains attainable reality to those whose faith
boy wishes to possess, boy, fearful
of reality collapsing in on him, perhaps, indeed,
a "coward," swims to bottom of Great Lake
and returns some time later as either a wolf
or a basketball player with a vertical leap
of forty-eight inches, the equivalence of a small child.

When Disaster Strikes 4

You may find yourself eating three
enormous meatballs and watching Korean soap
operas in the living room of a family you've never
met. An advertisement for an innovative
new hair removal product may come on.
You may be falling asleep when a cricket lands
on your mouth or eating five blueberry muffins
in somebody's kitchen after being awakened by
a conversation about an investment banker gone
wild. He may have killed his current family
as well as his previous one. You may be vomiting up
a Sprite at a Puffin Stop, or a raspberry sorbet
at Buddy's, or under a dock on your way to see
the puffins, or a few slices of pizza on the side
of South Orange Ave. The red and yellow
lights blur. You may have just thrown up
in front of the woman you love in Atlantic Highlands,
New Jersey. She won't know you love her.
Some guy may be throwing up on a Brooklyn
street corner, another guy running away.
You may be at the Irish Lion on a quiet Sunday
evening when someone screams out, Don't
fuck with it, shut your ass, at a woman before
storming across the street to an ATM.
Marc may make a joke about women's tennis
that you'll never be able to recreate accurately
for anyone. Nick will probably be pissed off
about something, most likely everything.
You may be in a Holiday Inn parking lot
on the hottest day of the year listening to the Pixies
and reading Dorothy Wordsworth's journals.
Can someone clear something up for me? What kind
of day can it possibly be when all William does

is gather sticks? And I quote: *Feb. 9*
William gathered sticks. I mean, come on,
WTF? Even I do more
than that in a day. Maybe you'll be
in Louisiana, maybe there'll be a woman made of sand.
Maybe Dave'll have sex with Mike's sister,
throw his mom's friend through a glass coffee
table after she tries to arrange a ménage à trois
between him, Brandon, and herself, maybe he'll join
the Navy, get married and have two
kids. Maybe he'll become an EMT.
Maybe he's got stories. Orange and blue,
bloody clothes, a Polaroid, telling Josh
his best friend is dead. Sour cream—
the perfect tribute to baked potatoes. You may
be missing Kitefest '99 or in the grocery store
at 6:30 on a Sunday morning buying
a chocolate milk, two air fresheners,
and a package of AA batteries.
Somewhere, casserole is getting cold, a book
is being thrown, a woman is crying and somewhere
else a man is eating tamales and a woman
is dancing in a kitchen with a burning napkin. A dog
is barking. It's about to rain. You may be eating
dried apricots in your underpants. You may
be accidentally stumbling upon a guy masturbating
in his Mercury Topaz outside a Red Lobster.
Maybe you'll be running from a spider, maybe
you'll be falling asleep in a park where someone
was murdered a week and a half ago. You may
be watching a Norwegian pulling his groin while
throwing a tire at the World's Strongest Man
Competition. Outside, somebody's shoveling snow.

You may be lying in bed at 1:30
on a Sunday afternoon watching *Wolfman: Legend
and the Science* and thinking, God, I hope nobody
drops by right now and catches me
in bed at 1:30 on a Sunday afternoon
watching *Wolfman: Legend and the Science*. You may
have just sat on a bee. You may have just
given a woman in a blue minivan terrible
directions because, really, you didn't know
what she was talking about, where she wanted
to go; you were just pretending. Isn't it wonderful
to pretend? Do you sometimes wish you could
pretend all the time? Like you've woken up
at eight o'clock on a Sunday morning with her
next to you, a sheet pushed aside exposing
one of her thighs, wind chimes outside
the window, a breeze coming in off the water
slapping waves up against the shore?
Like you don't have to get up day in and day out
alone and go to your job at the pharmaceutical
warehouse or delivering newspapers where
you'll end up driving around for over
an hour looking for a retirement community halfway
to Wayne so you can deliver a TV Guide.
Like you've never stood in a Wal-Mart parking
lot in late September with a woman you love
and the guy she loves and asked her to make
a decision and watched her walk away
with him. Like you've never had that five
minutes in late April when your friend's
gone to get something to eat and your favorite
television show is about to come on and you walk
to Bigfoot just after sunset to buy a Coke
or known that feeling of someone you love's breath

on your neck, her fingers on your cheek, only
to lose it. Like you've never driven all the way
to New Jersey to have a woman you love not
return your call when you get there. Like
you've never lost someone you've loved the day
she returned from Argentina, or the day you returned
from Mexico. Like you've never seen her in that blue
dress. Like she's never held you all night
in Michoacán. Like she never told you
she never wanted to speak to you again over the cold
hum of the air conditioner in her Toyota
in the parking lot of a bowling alley in the middle
of August. Milk and oil, blood and snow.
Like you wake up every morning, eat
toast and honey, scrambled eggs, blueberry
pancakes, and are about to drive to the airport
and get on a plane to California or Brazil or Portugal
to start over with new teeth and a new
shirt. It doesn't matter that you don't speak
Portuguese, you can pick up some tapes at the library
and learn it on the way. Just enough
to get by. And when the disaster strikes:
close your eyes, remember the last time
you'll ever see her, in the Cloverdale Burger King
parking lot, your sunburned feet, a pink
shirt, wait for the tone, then forget everything.

My Speech at a Local Campaign Rally

I'm voting for Don Simpson, not
because he's a Republican, but because he lives
up the road from Sarah. I like to speed
my vortex cube over the hill he lives at the top of
because I know it pisses him off and because,
honestly, it's none of his business how fast
I decide to go. Last summer he spray painted
SLOW DOWN in orange across the road.
For that I had to go twice as fast. But that's
good old Don. You see, he cares
about safety and safe driving. I'm voting
for Don Simpson because his lawn is an abandoned
junkyard. His brother lives in a habitrail
surrounding his cabin, they smash watermelons
in the street, and he's got a blue vortex
cube with an enormous antenna and a megaphone
strapped to the grill. And although I've never
been inside the Waffle House 3000, I imagine
when I see his car there late at night
he's toiling away at some legal papers,
rewriting the documents that'll determine the future
of this town. I guess that's what it all
boils down to here, folks: the future
of this town. And that's when you've got to ask
the question: who will best secure the future
of this town? A man like Paul McCartney?
He's not your man. He's a cheater, a crook,
a "bastard" if you will. What would good people
like yourselves want with a man like that?
You know, I've heard an occasional Saturday night'll
find him out wallowing in the pig farm or recording
a crummy new song with Quincy Jones
in his home studio or having sex with a mannequin.

That, my friends, is the real Paul McCartney. Don
Simpson is without a doubt your man. He comes
from a long line of local politicians,
including former county surveyor Liberace.
He's constantly patrolling out on Lance Armstrong
Memorial Thruway in Sector 118
of the Decorative and Commemorative Sword District
with his brother, assuring neighbors everything
is okay. And everything is okay with D.S.
He sells bunnies out of his backyard, he can fix
anything on a vortex cube, foreign or domestic.
He's out there, folks, and he knows
this town and what to do with it. He can shape
it into the community it once was: full of pride,
whole-heartedness, and sometimes in the fall
a little B-8-pumpkin-pie-bite-sized-capsule.
So, when you leap into that voting booth
come this November, I want you to remember
one name: Flashdance. I mean,
be serious, who would you rather have
guide us through the 21st century? A man
who loves to bathe himself in cream cheese,
or a responsible, God-fearing, mostly-clean
sex-lover with the drive and determination
to provide everyone with free green beans
at next year's Catfish Festival and bring
Norman Fell to next year's County Fair!

Bridgeton

Some would say I definitively grew up
that moment at age fourteen when, while
visiting a covered bridge festival in Bridgeton,
I watched my mother and father get mauled
by a huge, sideshow tiger that'd busted
loose when the sixteen-year-old kid
who'd been keeping an eye on the thing went
to make out with Tiffany Johnson behind
the Baptist church. Others would say I just
made that up right now to sound
interesting because sometimes I feel like
I really don't have any need to get
any ideas or feelings across aside from
the random observational quip here
and there and maybe an occasional slam at one
of my enemies. Like how I detest Julie Piepmeyer
and how great the name Bridgeton is for this
town because you can just imagine the settlers
back two hundred and fifty years ago
or whatever building this covered bridge and saying,
Well, we got this covered bridge, I guess
we might as well call this damn town
Bridgeton. I mean, we got nothing else
to call it do we? What are the other ideas?
Weedtown? Horseville? Grass City? I mean,
some other guy's already named this creek
Big Raccoon Creek and we don't want to live
in Big Raccoontown do we? That'd suggest
this town is overrun by big raccoons,
which would probably be detrimental to our tourism
industry because everybody'll just be like, Man, I'm not
going to Big Raccoontown, it's overrun
by a bunch of big scary raccoons. Though I guess

if the people thought the raccoons were friendly,
tourism would boom because everybody'd want
to see the big raccoons, have their pictures taken
with them and so forth, wouldn't they? Then I guess
we'd be a huge disappointment when all
these families come around in their station wagons
which will one day be invented, wearing
their outfits made entirely out of buffalo testicles.
We'd have to dress up in raccoon costumes
to please them, or I guess just kill them as they roll
into town. Anyway, all in favor of Bridgeton
say aye—and so it went. I just hope
the local Bridgeton historian never reads this
and gets offended (there's no way you're reading
this, are you? If you are, e-mail me),
because Bridgeton is really a nice town to spend
a few hours in, especially during
a covered bridge festival every fall, even though
the locals charge up to FOUR DOLLARS
for parking.

The Horse's Adventure

The horse discovered a gateway to another
dimension, and with nothing else to do, moseyed
into it just for grins, and man, you
don't even want to know what happened
next—it was just, like, Horse at the French
Revolution. Horse in Franco's living room.
Horse on the moon. Horse in a supporting role
in an episode of *ER*. Horse being shot
out of a cannon. Horse on *The Price Is Right*.
Horse in a Whitesnake video. Horse
at Kennedy's assassination. Horse in the Tet
Offensive. Horse at the Gap gawking at some
khaki pants. Horse in Julie Piepmeyer's
bathroom. Horse being tossed out of an airplane
with a parachute strapped to its back, plummeting
toward Nebraska. Horse on Capitol Hill
(Yes, I'd like the floor to recognize
the distinguished horse from Arizona). Horse
on the subway. Horse authorizing a peace treaty
between the U.S. and Iraq. Horse
in the Evansville State Hospital. Horse caught up
in a White Hen robbery. Horse in the Kentucky
Derby. Horse staring at the merry-go-round
at King's Island in Cincinnati, Ohio.
The list goes on and on. And so goes
the horse's adventure, where one minute
it's standing next to Pat Sajak and with a violent
flash like that of a murderous camera or the twirling
screen and music of a *Batman* episode
it's standing in the middle of US-23
with a screaming motorist speeding toward it.
And this horse, whirling through dimension
after dimension, spiraling carmines, suicidal

jasmines, and mathematical theorems tornadoing
past it, being placed in situation
after situation—what had it learned
when all was said and done and it was back
at Tom Wallace's farm? Nothing is better
than Rachel Wallace while they stand in the barn
in the middle of February and she draws pictures of it
to take to school tomorrow.

Marc McKee

Marc McKee has never participated
in a swimsuit competition, nor
has he used tongs for any purposes that weren't
medical related (to my knowledge). I've yet
to convince him of the brilliance of feedback,
the blurred water tower, the eight minutes
after sunset, or standing in a field in Quebec
without a French-speaking consort, only
a few lonely sheep, the rain beating
against a blue tarp. Marc McKee
divides his life into two categories: period
of debauchery and period of guilt following period
of debauchery, but most of the time I have trouble
distinguishing between the two, or, more
appropriately, figuring out when the first
ended and when the second began, because
often it seems that he's still floundering
in a period of debauchery, sleeping in one woman's
bed, then another's, then his own,
alone, then a married woman's. Yeah,
this saddens me a little, because I want him
to be happy and I can't be certain if he is, but before
you know it I'm in the checkout at the grocery
and remembering the need for Preparation H,
but it's too late to go back, the cashier
is hurrying me through, Will that be paper or plastic,
Thank you and Have a nice day, and then
I have to go to the laundromat, clean up
someone else's mess from a luncheon
with Bell Chevigny, make cheese sandwiches
from the trunk of my car and eat them in a liquor
store parking lot, all with my ass really burny.
If Marc McKee were required to list his likes

and dislikes for a beautiful bachelorette, it would go
something like this: likes: rainy days,
flannel sheets, candles, long walks
on the beach, horseback riding, the Indiana Pacers,
lobster, traveling, chocolate pudding, napping
with his cat Lucy, roller coasters, cuddling
by a fire, champagne, romantic comedies, Tito
Jackson, dancing. Dislikes: spiders, negative
people, pork, couch potatoes, dirty underpants,
religious discrimination. Marc McKee
was raised in Big Sandy, Texas, and lives
in Houston, though he's not a crime fighting hero,
not a member of an elite group of secret
agents, nor has he ever been required
to put out a small house fire with an outdated
extinguisher then afterwards repaint the kitchen
so his landlord won't notice. Marc McKee
has never leaned, nor loafed, nor invited, in any
sense of the word, his soul. Marc McKee
once won an entire collection of romance
novels at a Valentine's Day dance. He once
ate an olive out of someone's hand, once
fell in love with an older woman, once
spent an entire spring driving to
and from Washington, D.C. This was the spring
we met, the spring Sarah would leave me
then two days later sleep with me again,
the spring he never bought an art book,
the spring of rain and more rain and call
numbers smudged on notebook paper and buses
pulling away without someone who could have
done something, who could have done something
important if only that bus hadn't pulled away.

42

The spring of more rain and then grayness,
an orangish hue in the morning, the spring before
everything got all messed up because
of new zoning laws, before agendas
were established at town meetings, before
the discovery of remarkable new irrigation
techniques, before the construction of an interstate
had begun. The spring of some drunken mumbling
followed by a parking ticket, more
drunken mumbling and finally passing out
on the bedroom floor of a guy with an adult
baby fetish. Marc McKee has never
masturbated in his Honda Civic, nor
has he tried to have an argument with someone
about semantics after putting the better half
of a giant tootsie roll in his mouth. His call back
policy is erratic and he doesn't use the word
freaking as much as I do, but I don't hold that
against him. Plus, he's read Umberto Eco
and has a subscription to *Rolling Stone*. I don't
think he's ever been to Vancouver, but one
gorgeous May things were perfect and he flew
to San Francisco and I lied to his family, telling them
he was working at a video store. Sometimes,
maybe, things were too perfect, you think?
And then there was a long pause and everything
returned to how it was before, only someone
you once knew very well no longer
called and no longer had a role in your life.
Then you moved north. A slight motion
was made, sure, as if everyone was about
to applaud, but then moments later the motion
subsided and there was no applause, only
a ringing telephone, the flickering of a lamp, a moldy

davenport being tossed into a cornfield.
Sometimes, I'm afraid Marc McKee may drink
too much, but then other times
I think it may be that I drink too little,
or that I overanalyze the whole thing
because of the way I was raised. Then I forget
it all, then remember Kierkegaard: *Life*
can only be understood backwards; but it must
be lived forwards. And that just agitates me
to a point of intense vibration until I turn on
the television and watch beauty pageants and/or
country music award shows. Regardless,
Marc McKee has never lived in Mexico.
Marc McKee's mother was never arrested
for disorderly conduct, he's never held a woman
he's loved for the last time in the parking lot
of a fast food restaurant, not caring
that she never had her two front teeth,
because other things were always more important
than teeth. Her stationary, how she looked
in that black dress, how those letters somehow
got you through it all even though
her handwriting was almost completely illegible—
the mere notion that they could have said things like
I miss you, I love you, and I could never, ever
live without you, was always more

than enough.

Frida Kahlo

I've been to Coyoacán twice, but never
to Frida Kahlo's house—likewise, I've never
been to Madonna's house, but I did kiss
Jonathan's girlfriend in front of a Frida Kahlo
print, though I forget which one it was now.
And so, you're just dying to know what insights
I have about Frida Kahlo. That's right, you,
sitting there, in your dinosaur pajamas,
drifting into wondrous slumber as you read this,
you're absolutely dying to know how
I'm going to spin this wacky thing. Well, everyone's
got to mention the lachrymose existence,
the impalement, the suffering, Diego's mendacity,
etc. I've got to hand it to you, it's all there,
so what am I supposed to say about this woman
that hasn't already been said? I don't know,
but Margarita gave me a Diego Rivera
t-shirt I wear to bed, I can tell you that much.
It has a picture of him on it and says
Diego Rivera: Pintor Guanajuatense.
And Frida Kahlo, where is she? Oh,
maybe she's out back galloping around
with a deer body, licking casually the salt lick
we've left for her. Or smashing up on the grill
of a freaked out motorist on his way to St. Louis
for an emerging markets convention—not only
did he nail a deer, it had the freaking head
of a woman for God's sake. Or maybe she's walking
unknowingly into a hunting area, men
in camouflaged jackets and orange caps
peering down at her through their rifle scopes
from the majestic oaks. That damn thing's
got the head of a woman, they'll think, right

before opening fire. Just think about it,
man, to have Frida Kahlo's head
mounted above your fireplace, you'd be the talk
of the town. The thing I want to know is what
happened to the deer head? Somewhere there's some
perplexed accountant in a cubicle wearing dumb
suspenders and a stupid tie with a deer head.
His coworkers are just like, What the hell
happened to you Mike, you look terrible. He won't
speak, though, and with the brain of a deer
will just jump around the office from Xerox
to fax machine in utter bewilderment. The computer
will scare the hell out of him, but there'll be
nowhere to run. Mike the Deer Man.
He'll be out on the racquetball court that evening
jumping around senselessly, knocking that blue
ball all over the place and end up jumping
in his BMW 328i and flying
out to the country after the moonrise to curse
Frida Kahlo and the poems about her. What's happened?
Where's my poem? he'll scream. Look at me.
Will somebody please look at me?

Readings

What I want to know is who's the idiot
who said no when Michael Ondaatje asked
if there was an echo in the room during his reading,
the idiot who said we could hear him just fine,
because all I heard was a series of mumbles
and a lot of s sounds which for some reason
made the audience laugh every now
and then, which, in turn, I guess, made
me feel like I was missing out
on the "big joke," like when you're standing around
with a group of sophisticated punsters and they're all
in a cock-a-hoop over Teebob's remark
about the corduroy pillow's recent appearance
in all the newspapers and you just don't *get* it.
Public readings, really, are weird
if you think about them. I mean, I suppose
I enjoy them about as much as anybody, but why?
I already know how to read, I've never needed
anybody to read to me except when I was a kid
and needed my mom to read *The Little Raccoon*
to me night after night, and I probably haven't
enjoyed readings to that extent ever since,
possibly because she could get through the entire
book in one sitting, or possibly because
I got to lie in a bed, I'm not sure.
But even if we did all get to lie
in beds at public readings I probably still wouldn't
enjoy them as much, especially fiction readings
which are difficult for me because the reader usually
reads portions of his big book and gives
unhelpful summaries of each portion's context
within the rest of the novel. Case in point,
Rick Moody. I mean, when he ripped

into that whosoever chapter of whatever book
that's from, I was about three centimeters
from causing a scene, let me tell you, and there's no
telling what that would've entailed, most likely
a chair flying through the air and some kind
of goat-headed shriek emanating from deep
within me. I just think Michael Ondaatje
could've used the echo to his advantage, that's all,
because echoes can be a good thing, especially
if you're trapped in a small canyon near
the Ohio River in the dead of summer—when
you cry out, How do I get the hell out of here?
a passerby up top has three or four
opportunities to try to understand
what you just screamed and when he answers
you have three or four opportunities to hear
his reply. I mean, he could've at least treated it
like a huge-venued rock concert or something—
thrown on some leather pants and maybe
broken a guitar over the podium while screaming,
Ladies and gentlemen, are you ready
for some poetry?

Other Readings

Not that I meant to, like, go off
on Rick Moody or anything, it was just
that his whosoever chapter of whatever
book that's from felt unbearably monotonous,
for Koo too, because we were both just like
Come on, man, get to the freaking point,
although "man" and "freaking" are more
my appropriations. I mean, just imagine
if I started up a whosoever sequence
right now, like whosoever has set a ravine
on fire during the January snowstorm,
whosoever has ever left a bunch
of starfish to die in a Mexican sink, whosoever
once found a diary in a hotel room
and began reading it to see who it belonged to,
whosoever realized it belonged to Candice
at the very moment she bopped in the door
after an invigorating swim in the pool, whosoever
once found himself in the back seat
of a Thunderbird at one in the morning
nursing a broken hand, whosoever
spilled an entire pitcher of pink lemonade
on himself at Easter dinner, whosoever
has felt a terrible loneliness in the car wash,
whosoever heard a woman outside the Italian
restaurant begin a sentence with, I'm going
to write a letter to the editor, whosoever
is married to that woman, whosoever is tired
of hamburgers with zany names, whosoever finds it
embarrassing to ask a waitress for a J.R. Ewing,
or ask anyone for that matter, whosoever finds
the name Olde English Burger ridiculous,
whosoever doesn't want to be reminded

of a time of hierarchical feudalism and the plague
while eating dinner, whosoever has just
tooled around Canada for about a half
hour—God, it's really monotonous, isn't it?
And I bet you're just sitting there thinking,
Man, why won't he just get to the freaking
point, only perhaps using your own adjectives,
like, if you're creative, you may be saying Pointer,
why doesn't he just get to the pointy point
and perhaps you, too, are seconds away
from flying into your own cyclone of violence.
Regardless, you get the picture. And his list
seemed a lot more drab and darker, like it may
have contained a lot of violet scenery and depressing
clothes and eye makeup, but I can't quite
remember. I'm not saying he's a bad reader
or anything either, mind you; in fact, you might
even say just being remembered,
for whatever reason, is better than not
being remembered at all. Take Ralph Burns,
for instance. I can't remember anything about
his reading, except that I think he was wearing a brown
blazer, but even that I'm not a hundred
percent on—probably the reason for that, though,
isn't reading-related at all, but moreso
the fact that, at the time, I was kind of
preoccupied with the idea that all our thoughts
about bottled water and peanut butter cups
are pretty ridiculous considering our impending
deaths.

Summer

If you ever eat too many enchiladas,
don't go over to your ex-girlfriend's apartment
immediately afterwards, rip off your pants
and have sex with her, because unbelievable
cramps will be the least of your problems.
As will be the missing geography book,
the yellow sweater, the quarter on the floor,
the poorly contrived story of the horror film,
the kid pretending to die in a lecture hall,
the teens riddled by the opposite sex and beer,
being popular and "fitting in," the blood
on the wall, in the parking garage, all over
the sweet, sweet leather interior of the Mercedes,
the hopeless security guard, the college campus
locked in a maelstrom of hardcore partying
and being murdered. As will be the neighbors
drunk in the hot tub again, the abundance
of swans over here, the lack of swans there,
the time you didn't go to Guadalajara,
the Fourth of July you spent in Pátzcuaro where
Orlando, drunk, swam around in a putrid
fountain and got typhoid, the Fourth of July
you spent in love with a woman who didn't love you,
the Fourth of July you spent working at Dairy Queen.
As will be the giant alligator crashing
the CEO's big party, your declaration
as you crossed the Delaware River to never enter
the state of New Jersey again so help you God,
the new mall being built up north,
the old mall's progressing unpopularity,
the distant sounds of chain saws and barking
dogs in the afternoon, the train flying
past the Mexican restaurant the two of you

walked out of, each of you unaware
of the future, unaware that a man your mother
loves is the engineer, that weeks later
his train will derail en route to Kansas City,
unaware that the horse has been sold because
she was just too much to handle. As will be
the time the Ford twins stole your pants and shirt
out of your gym locker and wore them to school
the next day, the night two years ago you spent
with your crotch up to a public restroom dryer
in a vain attempt to dry yourself off as a five
year old boy made fun of you
after she spilled a tall glass of ice cold
Coca-Cola in your lap. As will be
everything—up to and including that moment:
the egg salad at the Finnish restaurant, the guy
at the grocery with Mr. T hair, the twelve
Boy Scouts from Milwaukee about to die
in a van accident, the young girl there
on the street who believes she has a grasp
on it all, but, really, may never know what it's like
to feel happiness, who'll sleep around and change
hairstyles often and wear depressing clothes
trying to fill this void. As will be
your ex-girlfriend's request afterwards, despairing,
that you promise never to mention this
to anyone, and your promise.

No, the bulk of your problems will be jammed
into a file marked "you" by some junior
executive in development who requests
that you sort it all out for the big meeting
Thursday. You know, give it some kind

of logical order, make it presentable, maybe
utilize some overheads, graphs, pie charts,
that kind of thing. Your real problems involve
rearranging everything that's happened in the last
twenty some odd years and making
some kind of sense of it all. But that's impossible.
Leave that for some virgin dynamo,
somebody who enjoys order, who enjoys a cut
and dried scenario where A plus B equals C,
who actually believes the stuff that happens
is linked nicely together with guitar interludes
like the comedy bits on a Bill Hicks album.
But for me, it just doesn't work that way.
I mean, some things just don't make sense—
like why I love Broadway ever so very much
or why I've listened to the first three minutes
of "I Am the T-Rex" for the past two
and a half hours or what my dream about the nativity
scene down at the town hall means.
I mean, what it actually *means*. No,
the bulk of your problems won't be easily solved
and if you're anything like me you'll long
for the summer even though you detest hot
weather—because right now there could be nothing
better, right now there could be nothing better
than lying in bed in late afternoon by an open
window somewhere in the middle of nowhere
with someone you love in the next room
and a dog pressed up beside you, asleep.
And let me just say, when that
cold front comes through like it always will
and one of those thunderstorms to end all
thunderstorms appears where one minute

you're looking off to the west saying, Yeah, looks like
we're about to get a big one and the next
you're watching the neighbor's barn get bashed
into pieces by a tornado and the neighbor's cat,
Mr. Scrambles, get struck by lightning—whatever
you do, don't freak out when at 11:30
the electricity is restored and your answering
machine begins playing every message it's ever
recorded since its creation on July 3, 1987.

The Right Hand of Karma Is Extending Its Middle Finger

The day I stepped onto an elevator
with the fiancé of the woman I had an affair with
a month earlier I was oblivious, thinking
he was just some sociopath unfamiliar
with the norms of elevator riding—you know,
like it's improper when riding an elevator
with another person to stand only eight
inches away, torso a'glisten with animalistic
hatred: you may be threatening that other
individual's personal space. But see, he knew
me, I didn't know him, and even if I did
I was too excited about this copy
of Victorian erotica I'd discovered minutes
earlier to notice. Let's face it, peeps, I've
been living in a world parallel to this one, a few
spaces off to the side, cylindrical and madly
geometric, waiting for a nice tornado to toss me
into some trailer park just over the horizon
into the recesses of insanity—because come on,
it's so much nicer than facing
that insolent browbeater reality—so much easier.
I used to know this guy who'd douse himself
with Right Guard and light himself on fire.
How wonderful it'd be to be that guy,
to admit you're an animal, that you've just given up
and no longer want to exist in a civilized
society. And how we'd all laugh at him, and cuss,
bawdy gentlemen worshipping that
to which we would never succumb. So I guess this
is my note of resignation, my finality—
you win, world, I'm all out of ideas.
Everyone on the golf course looks exactly

like my college Calculus teacher and I don't know
what the hell I'm supposed to do.

While Anne Reads a Lengthy Poem About Her Grandmother's Funeral and Our Mortality

I'm reminded of some details Bill told me
about his aunt's funeral in Memphis a few years
ago—a paraplegic whose casket somehow
got tipped on its side while being lowered
into the grave during a thunderstorm. The pallbearers,
Bill included, were forced into the mud
in an attempt to turn the casket right side
up, digging and clawing their way in and out
of the hole, slopping around for an audience
of bereft women in black dresses and red
hats. Finally they gave up and left her
on her side, creeping away in their Cadillacs and ruined
suits, the wives angry at the husbands. I once
watched a funeral procession from the window
of a monastery in Valenciana. It was June
and hadn't rained in a while—only a few
men carried the casket past a green
wall that read TODOS SOMOS RESPONSABLES
in white. There were no spectators, only a girl
peeling an orange, selling silver necklaces
which dangled and chimed in the breeze. Death, for me,
has become a bloated and muted thing—a fish
about to explode, even if you die during a rock
concert or in a Japanese execution chamber.
Like TV static, it's foreboding—an 18
wheeler hauling Little Debbie snack cakes up I-75
late at night. Anne seems to think death
is more about food and family gathering to mourn
and question our own mortality while eating ham
and deviled eggs on a red and white tablecloth,
but I fell asleep at my grandfather's
service and afterwards ate a cheese

omelet at Round the Clock. I've only thought
about dying on the subway, on the bus in Newark,
or in Mexican taxis with brightly colored pictures
of the Virgin of Guadalupe on the dash. I think
maybe that's what the picture's there for—to repent
right before you die in the mountains. I was always
going to repent just before I died, but what if
I die suddenly and can't—what if I could
but didn't know who to repent to? I'm afraid
of what exactly my final thoughts will be:
all the time I spent by the microwave
and toaster in this empty kitchen, the last time
Sarah came on to me—her hand
down my pants while I had the jingle for Ted's Aqua
Marine in my head, the black and white cat
that rubbed up against my leg at the Lincoln
Cabin, a sign on US-41 reading
PRISON AREA, DO NOT PICK UP HITCHHIKERS.
Anne's poem has ended and I give up
on death; I only want to mention a survey
I got in the mail a few days ago
which asked this question: Do you believe
in immortality, if you take this to mean
the continued existence of the individual soul
after the end of organic life?

No Story, Just a Comment on Some of Anne's Poems

I think Anne feels inclined to write poems
about living in a small town, which I don't
mind. They contain curious details about cows
during thunderstorms, an orange pickup
pushed into an abandoned quarry, neglected cats
shot in the head, and a tornado tossing a schoolbus
over a bridge on Wylie Road. I get
annoyed, however, when they go on
about drunken hard-ass fathers, teachers
beating kids, and a dead body in a barn.
You see, too much has happened in small
towns during the last fifty years, and we're
constantly working to cover it all up,
throw some wet leaves and moss over a dead
girl, that sort of thing. Like the Klan: we deny
its existence but know it's there, in some barn
or hollow out on a county road and way
back past some barbed wire fence.
Anne's poems expose everything sour.
For instance, if she had written this she'd have
described the dead girl—slashed at the neck,
cold and blue, missing fingernails, blood
soaked underwear around her ankles. That's where
she goes wrong because it's not all bad.
I've been denying everything for years now.
Anne doesn't see that not every
story should be told, even if it happened to you.
For instance, once I was wasted over at Dave's
while a dog was barking in his driveway.
Dave got pissed, took out his crossbow
and shot a blunt arrow into the dog's
side, making him howl instead of run away.
We got paranoid and hid in a closet, thinking

the cops would come by, see this dog
with an arrow in its side yelping in the driveway,
bust in and arrest us. Instead, the arrow
fell out, the dog disappeared,
and a few hours later the woman across the street
found her husband in the front seat of his car
holding a gun to his head, threatening to kill
himself.

The Year of Living Regrettably

That was the year the woman you loved
left you standing alone in a Wal-Mart
parking lot, the year you spent in central
Mexico, the year you saw too much
of I-70 after midnight and highway 46
after three, the year of ten thousand deaths,
the year clouds rose so high
and the sky became so yellow you thought
this must be the end, this has to be
the end—but it wasn't, and each morning
you'd wake at 5:30 and drive
from Bloomington to Indianapolis to survey
the damage, the housing communities destroyed,
the trees uprooted and everyone still alive
after all these years. Today is Rosetta
Lee Southerland Pippenger's one hundredth
birthday and she doesn't know any
of this. Lord knows she's lived on a farm
outside Grubbs, Arkansas, with her family
most of her life. She doesn't even know
what Bloomington in early March feels like,
the sky so dark and the wind emerging from so
far overhead, then falling downward toward
South Walnut where you walk amongst
the traffic and the people moving this way
and that, marrying, forming bands, practicing
in the basement. It's like this feeling, this desire
to get in your car and drive to Georgia and keep
going until you've forgotten everything
that's ever happened, everything you've ever
known—that summer you dragged Sarah's
dog up from the road and buried him,
that summer you asked her to marry you

in Knoxville, that summer she won't remember
because of you, but because of the guy
she left you for, that summer was hot, wasn't it,
and you'd only know later it'd be the dog's
last. Rosetta Lee Southerland Pippenger has 21
grandchildren, 45 great-grandchildren,
and 41 great-great-grandchildren.
Yes, that's quite a bit of procreation,
though I bet she never found herself sitting
on Laura's bathroom floor one Halloween
in Chicago amidst the lime green frog decor
thinking, Dear God, I've got to think
of a way out of this mess, I don't belong here.
A danceable melody, maybe. I've never
told anyone this, but I almost couldn't
take it anymore the night of the prom—
her sequined dress, beautiful hair,
and insistence that I didn't love her
were too much to handle. It was prom
night for God's sake and Jennifer Wilson
had eaten my raspberry tort without asking.
This is visiting your hometown for a week;
this is longing to be back in that mess,
before the ice has melted and the swans
have returned, before the summer people
come back with their aquatic apparatuses
and custom vans. This is a balcony, heat
and sitting beside the Ohio River with someone
you love, listening to her laugh at the name
of a bizarre refreshment. This is driving to Ypsilanti
to visit Anne, this is a wrathful God,
this is what we go through, the owls at two
in the morning, the deer looking at you through

the front window, your mother and father asleep
upstairs in their separate rooms. This is eating
too much Indian food and spending an entire
evening trying to recover. This is falling
asleep in the park every day before
delivering newspapers. This is indigo,
a choreographed step, a glass of wine,
and finally, in the end, erupting into a rage
and walking out of a bar around four AM.
Dear Dave, I've finally found that place to buy
athletic shoes without being hassled
by track and field failures in referee jerseys, where
they actually have your size and the salesmen
don't come back out with two
boxes saying, Well, we've got a size
four and a size eighteen, sometimes they run
a little big you know so these babies
might fit you, but there's no way
a shoe eight sizes too small
is going to fit you and shoe buying has always
been so horrible hasn't it, because in junior
high if you only owned one pair
of shoes you were hassled by guys named
Shane or Adam who were football stars
but by the time you graduated
high school had become dust and escaped
through the ventilation system,
out into the world where we all breathe Shanes
and Adams every day, which may be why
we're sometimes cruel even when
we don't want to be, why we may get
upset at four in the morning in Detroit and why
we yell at people we love over the phone

when they tell us they never want to speak
to us again. All you know
is someone is crying and now is not the time
to have a conversation about a pre-war
Britain. Right now I wonder if Rosetta
Lee Southerland Pippenger has ever been
in a sewing club, ever discussed true
left-handed knitting at a local bookstore
while you and I leaf through books
about people named Jawaharlal and Eric,
and right now I doubt she's ever participated
in an egg tossing competition in a swimsuit
or had a gallon of ice dumped on her while
lounging beside the Pacific Ocean. And the feeling
of walking out of that bookstore is so
wonderful, the yellowness of the street lights
so close to perfect, so close
to perfect—like resting on the couch on a spring
afternoon, the windows open, the raccoon down
by the rowboat and your cat beside you, eyes
closed—never wanting the moment to end.
The place you once called home, the place
you felt most comfortable, the place you loved
Sarah and lost and loved again is now the one
place that seems foreign to you. It's like driving
north on I-69 on a Friday afternoon
and noticing a sign that says FOR TRAFFIC INFO,
TURN TO 530 AM, not seeing
any traffic and turning on the radio
only to hear someone talking about you.

Desperation

Let's just pretend the brown shirt
that used to cause such a commotion on the dance
floor of your life never shrunk
in the wash and you don't have days now
where every shirt you put on
looks like it was knitted by some delusional
grandmother who thinks your name is Kevin
and is one of those grandmothers who actually
never learned how to knit, or at least
knit properly, because everything she knits
has four arms or two neckholes
or no holes at all, as if she were knitting
for monstrous, mutant grandchildren
or giant Zynobots with names like Kevin—
which could be a good thing if you think
about it because it means she considers
you not only some giant Zynobot
because of the fact she calls you Kevin
and knits you improper, problematic
clothing which makes you uncomfortable all
day, but her giant Zynobot, which makes
you feel loved and good even though
the grandmother knitting clothing for you
doesn't know your name and isn't even
your grandmother for that matter. It's like
your 28-year-old neighbor
who apparently enjoys walking around her kitchen
in the nude fresh out of the shower—it makes
you feel good, but weird, like you may
have evolved into some kind of peeping
tom (that's right, I'm talking about you,
Tom Piepmeyer). To avoid loneliness, dress
comfortably, wear sensible shoes, to fall

in love with an orange dress and the woman
who fits it perfectly—this is what it's all about
in the end. I mean, look at it this
way. Look at how the man buys
his microwave dinner and pays the gorgeous
cashier in quarters. Look at how much
pepper he uses on the meals he prepares for himself.
Look at how much gin and tonic
he drinks during the Super Bowl right before
he calls you and asks you to come over,
right before he falls into the pool
after dark. Look at how the athletes dump
Gatorade on one another, on the coaching
staff. Look at the cashier's metallic blue
fingernails and try not to think
about how you want to come back around
after her shift ends and take her home
with you like in the movies. Or, look
at the hush that befell the student body
in the gymnasium in Big Sandy, Texas,
that moment just before Armando Martinez
punched Ricky Sampson with all his strength
in the back.

Apocalypse

If eating corndogs and watching the demo-
lition derby on TNN
Friday nights is a sign of the apocalypse,
then the end of the world is certainly being birthed
in my living room. But I shouldn't run away from it
like actors from computer simulated dinosaurs,
instead I should welcome it with open
arms and a smile, take it home and give it
a name—Pupipo or Chad. After all, it needs
love and acceptance just like anyone.
Think about it, how would you feel if everyone
feared your impending arrival? If The Iceman
tried to disguise his voice whenever you called
and everyone on the camping trip sat around
the campfire drinking hot beer trying
to get so drunk they wouldn't notice
your presence? You'd feel pretty rotten,
wouldn't you? So I'm saying, don't
abandon the apocalypse at Porko's house
in Pittsburgh and get a ticket while speeding away
in Zanesville, Ohio. I mean, Porko's
no child caregiver, he's an auto mechanic
for Christ's sake—he'll fix your VW but not
your life. Give it some time to grow, you'll
realize everything will have been worthwhile.
By junior high it'll be going steady with girls,
playing football and baseball and golf every
day, shoving the heads of unsuspecting
nerds into toilet bowls. You'll see, by
high school it'll be dating a cheerleader
named Crystal and be captain of the football
team. It'll finally get that Firebird
working. It'll graduate, go to technical
college, flunk out, get a job

at the alignment place west of town, spray
paint Crystal Hudson's name on an overpass
just before she leaves it for a guy who repairs
small engines at Rick's Small Engine
Repair. It'll spend its nights on the back porch
drinking Wild Turkey and Old Milwaukee,
pining for the good old days. Pretty
soon everything will begin to fall apart—
it'll be buying more and more shotguns
and stashing them in the closet, talking about
our right to bear arms. It'll start saying
backwoods militia groups make a lot of sense.
That's when everything will go down. You'll
be sitting around one afternoon
watching *Mama's Family* because it's on
Channel 2 and Channel 2 is the only
channel you get, and everything prophesied
will erupt. Most will die. And you'll be one
of the last remaining, driving down I-64
in a white Toronado, turning the radio
to AM 1610 for some
information—weather, tourism, fishing,
you won't care. You'll be searching for an off-track
wagering facility to put 500 dollars
down on inescapable death and end up
at a British Petroleum in Burnt Prairie, Illinois,
refueling and cleaning your windshield in silence,
a Ford Aerostar on either side of you
filled with men staring at you, mumbling
to one another in Spanish.

Hell

I wouldn't be surprised if some oratorical
dynamo were to describe Hell as a place where
your favorite television program is pre-
empted by baseball every week
and you wind up passed out on the floor
after a night of watching cat documentaries
on four different channels
simultaneously, or a region where you
end up in one of the area's
top five romantic restaurants blowing a
fourth of your week's salary on food
whose only desire it seems at the time
is to be rolled up in the complementary
bread and eaten like a burrito. The next
thing you know you're walking out
of the concert like you're escaping the bad smell
of Terre Haute or a girl who stalked you
from Terre Haute and find yourself in a bar
where some woman in a poorly fitted, extremely
troublesome sweater hands you a cocktail napkin
with her phone number and the words *carpe diem*
scrawled across it. So you walk fourteen blocks to a party
only to be cornered most of the night by a Chinese
lawyer instead of that quintessential babe
you'd been hoping for, which in turn sends
you home where you stand in front of the sink
scraping dog excrement from the bottom of your shoe
with a butter knife before crawling into bed
and crying yourself to sleep. Yeah, it could
be that. Or it could be the place where
you find yourself helplessly watching
a seventy-year-old, white-haired woman
tumble down a hill toward a river.
She could be your grandmother. It could be
this movie theater where you see Rhubarb

and his swirly arm at the popcorn stand
waving his moose poem at you, making
incoherent references to snack cakes, you could be
gnawing at the delicious grasshoppers when in
walks the woman you love with your old college
roommate—you know, the guy who enjoyed
wrestling llamas and throwing ham radios
and tackleboxes out the window—telling you
all about the amazing sex they just had
in the storeroom of the Country Junction.
It's possible it could involve remembering
your father's birthday was yesterday while Tim
O'Brien reads and repeats how he's
from Minnesota in front of the home repair
section of the local bookstore while this guy
next to you is completely soused
and bumping into you every twenty
seconds. It could be a lot of things. Poems
that begin with long sentences and end with shorter
ones. Metapoemas of the Golden Age.
Getting stuck with Canadian money. Having
your wallet stolen at Space Camp. Being
trapped in Nepal with horrifying diarrhea
while a tiger circles the outhouse. Losing
your virginity on the hood of a Pontiac like Tim
O'Brien. Feeling the need to dominate your pets like
the cat documentaries say males tend
to do. Hell could be all these things
wadded into a pink box and delivered to you
by an old man with goggles riding a bicycle
from the fifties, but most likely it involves
driving down the highway being repeatedly
bitten by a mosquito with "Pike County Breakdown"
blaring from the stereo, altogether disbelieving
the existence of love.

Intramural Correspondence

I said for the sake of everything it's the hottest
night of the summer and you're in that Southern
motel with a hole in the wall for an air conditioner
again, and instead of receiving that call
from the front desk saying, Jesus, did we
put you in that room with no air conditioner?
the call's from me and I don't know you yet
but I need to tell you this. I said I need
to say how difficult things are
these days and because you're lying there
in the dark, like me, I know you'll understand.
I said as far as the trip from Bloomington
to Memphis and back is concerned, I never made it
out of Illinois and I was alone. But that's beside
the point. I said two springs ago,
two springs ago the world fell apart
but what was I to do aside from drive
through southern Illinois and say something
about lawn ornamentry. It's all a terrible cycle.
I said everything breaks down all
the time and how do people deal with it? I'd like
to know, wouldn't you? I said when I was five
my mother tore me from bed late at night
screaming at my father, a horrible motion was made,
glass broken. I said winter in Thunder Bay,
that's where I should be. I'm not in love
with myself but I'd like to know what it's like. I said
I'm tired. I said I'd like to drive a confidence-
inspiring car. I said the swans. The swans
are beautiful. I said everything will have changed
if I ever go home again. I said the blue
wavy girl. I said Kirk and I must have had that
we didn't see any impressionistic art

look all over our faces. How else would she
have known? I said it's impossible to rock a room
thoroughly if you get up there dressed as a flower
and begin your song with I'm a flower, in case
you were wondering. I said what's this all about?
I said the spring two years ago. I said
my mother went to jail. I said I miss her.
I said something about Wisconsin and loneliness
made me break down and cry that summer
afternoon while driving downtown and I can't
figure out why. I said something
about the circularity of things and this only
makes it more painful. I said on the train
with her head on my lap, why couldn't that train
never have stopped? I said she held my hand
in New York City, a city I hated.
I said only this makes me happy. But I don't
know what this is. I said this is enough,
enough for now, but is it? I said
we were chemistry lab partners and I fell
in love. I said where are you tonight, are you asleep
already, or have you had too much to drink?
I said do you ever feel like this, do you
ever just sit there and think this is it,
these are the things I have? I said have you ever
driven back from Terre Haute at three AM

with a bashed hand and blood all over your floorboard?
I like to use soaps at other people's
houses because other people always have such
fragrant, apricotish soaps and I like
to smell like apricots. I said I never made it
out of Illinois. I said what made me go back,
why did I ever plan to go back? Why didn't I

just go all the way to Mexico and never come back?
But I did both, went to Mexico and came back.
My father went away for four weeks and returned
home better. Is that it? I said why
do these things happen? Avocados
and white shirts and Q-tips and uncomfortable
bus rides to the Pacific Ocean. I said
if Christ came tomorrow, what
would you do today? Nothing will ever balance out.
I said I'd like to buy a vowel. I'd like
to buy an A please. I'm sorry, there are no
As. Sure, there are perfect moments, I named one
earlier: the train. Also, Mount St. Helen's,
Michoacán, falling asleep on Sarah's bed
three summers ago. I said I could go on,
I could continue forever like this, but I can't
figure out what it is I'm doing anyway. I said
I wish everything could be as simple and wonderful
as the hour's worth of church bells each
evening in the mountains of central Mexico. I said
where are you, or was it where am I.
I said people kill themselves each day,
like Dave's neighbor, or Chris's mom. I said
it's a terrible cycle. I said I never made it out
of Illinois. I said if I'd only made it,
if I'd only kept going. I said that summer
was the summer. Driving to Sarah's every
night. I said all you and I need is someone.
I said what are we doing? I said I can't
believe this drugstore stays in business,
Kirk said the directions for these earplugs are way
too complicated. I said I should save this Twinkie
for later because I know I'll be hungry.

And I was. I said thanks for calling the night
that tornado touched down two blocks away.
I said I hadn't known. I said I still
love her. I said something about an abortion.
I said my mother went to jail. I said
my mother won't ask people questions
because she's afraid. I said I'm afraid. I said
I don't know what's going on anymore.
I said I'm not in love with myself. I just want
to understand things is all. I said what's going on,
what am I doing. I said I asked her to marry me
in Tennessee. I said it's a terrible cycle
and I never made it out of Illinois, I said
what are you doing there, in that motel room
with no air conditioner, lying there, alone,
when I'm up here, and I'm always up here.
You said but I don't know you, it's late, and I may
never even see the real Mexico.

Werewolves

So I was thinking, werewolves are funny,
unless you're being chased by one, because
how many situations have you been in
where you wanted to A) turn into
a werewolf and tear apart the guy
talking about Flaubert or B) see
a werewolf charge out of the shadows,
tear apart the guy talking about Flaubert,
and disappear into the opposite shadows. If
B) were to happen, you'd just be
standing there thinking Jesus, what
the hell did I just see, I mean,
what was that thing; and take A) for example,
you'd probably be alone in the bathroom
after making such a fresh, exuberant kill
examining your paws thinking Jesus, what
the hell's happening to me? And just as
you're staring dumbfoundedly at yourself
in the mirror, noticing your fur and its stark
contrast to your Lands' End plaid shirt
and chinos you hear a toilet flush and out
of a stall steps a guy in a Lotus Festival
t-shirt who just wrote a novel
about existentialism, so you'd have to kill
him too. I suppose A) in the end
would have more drawbacks than B)
because it most likely would involve some
kind of desperate run out to the country
to a secluded barn or sheep shelter where
you attempt solitude or the companionship
of a bunch of sheep while a group of enraged,
gun crazy citizens have gathered half
a mile away to comb the area, sift

you out and blow you away with the old
silver bullet. There's also the possibility
of a stolen ambulance thrown in there
somewhere and a dedicated sheriff spouting off
advice on the Channel 2 News about what
to do if you see a werewolf. But then
you realize, as do the sheep, that you're
a wolf now and you love to eat sheep
and they become frightened, baaing
in terror as you rip into them as if they were part
of some fabulous all-you-can-eat buffet.
Then farmer Larry hears all this racket
you and the sheep are making, runs out
there, sees you cutting into his blue
ribbon prized possessions and bounds back
to the farmhouse to call the sheriff and grab
his smoothbore shotgun. You catch
a glimpse of him and head for the forest,
smashing into a petrified motorist on the way
before limping wounded into the brush, where
you curl up and pass away peacefully
or make one final attempt at killing
somebody, leaping hopelessly, arms
and legs fully extended, at a rookie deputy
as he pumps shots into your chest. It'd be
a shame to ruin such an expensive, plaid shirt
this way, but what would be even worse
is if Martin Sheen were somehow involved
with the TV movie version of your story,
playing, say, the college professor who's
an expert on werewolves and werewolf
history to the point that he's quoting medieval
rumors about eastern European wolf creatures

and 19th-century tales of mysterious
wolves somewhere in the Appalachian
Mountains; or the dedicated mayor who
wants to keep his town safe, but when
we get to know him we learn that he's also
an avid butterfly collector/electric
train hobbyist/family man who's primary
concern is to protect his wife and kids from werewolf
attacks. Of course it'd be painfully obvious
that the werewolf in this sense would represent
America's fear of the rise of lawlessness
and infidelity, and his desire to keep his close-knit
farming community safe from the werewolf
is really a desire to keep sex and violence
from spreading into the town he grew up in, played
little league Jai Alai in and kissed
Debbie Reynolds in—the town he cares
about. It'd be similar to the reverend's hatred
for dancing in *Footloose* maybe, only
in this case there'd be no DJ
ripping out top-forty hits
while a crowd of pubescent werewolves break
into one of the most unspeakable bourrées
ever witnessed after the new wolf-
boy in town just proved himself
by winning a game of chicken on a John Deere
tractor as some yokel out tedding
a field looked on in horror. It'd be
okay, though, if somebody like Rob
Lowe played you. You think he
could pull off the right combination
of haughtiness, bloodlust, and anguish
that seemed to define you during this difficult
time in your life.

You Won't Believe What's Happening in Hamtramck

Nor will you believe that your cat whom
you'd presumed male is actually female
and quite possibly pregnant. She's on the couch
now but dang, it's been quite a ride
hasn't it? Seventy-six degrees
and now this, a twirlyness nothing but
cloud-like, urgent motions made
from the balcony, a woman crying out No,
no, this is all wrong, this isn't
like Philadelphia at all. And somewhere
amongst the havoc, a Farfisa organ.
You've searched every nook and cranny
for that letter from Jenny and it's nowhere
to be found. (This is the point
where we can't hear little Billy Peterson's
cries from seat R-22, WHO
DO WE KNOW NAMED JENNY? due
to the outrageous saxophone solo). Nor
will you believe you actually ran
from the cops Friday night or that you
found yourself in your front yard at six AM
in your underpants, hopelessly thrashing
a broom about in an attempt to do something,
something indescribable maybe, maybe
ineffable or sublime—yes, there you were
under the big maple as dawn approached
striking out at the sublime. (This is the point
where Jinx, a mischievous, wise-cracking robot
with a heart enters the room and amuses us
with his hilarious antics). You won't believe
that nothing was revealed that you didn't know,
that no apples fell, that the music became louder
as you turned the corner, or that the night could be

like this: windy and so dark
and hot that you wake the next morning having
strained a muscle in your right leg. You won't
believe Cincinnati's chances for the national
championship at this point either, speaking
of legs, nor will you believe you can get
these extraordinary geegaws for such a low,
low price. Apparently Craig changed
his name to Spirit Wolf back in '97.
You won't believe what's happening with the woman
you love, the way a night in the mountains
can envelop you as you search for a lost wallet
and the snow begins to fall, how she sends
you a letter saying, This is all we have
in this terrible world and this is the sound the cat
makes behind the venetian blinds, how
the leaves appear so rapidly each spring
and then all of a sudden it's summer and you
don't know what you're going to do
with the box of kittens in your linen closet.
You won't believe this is it,
that this is what we have, that your inabilities
spring from a lack of communication
skills, that everyone thinks you're a jerk
down at the YMCA and that often
you don't feel like you have anyone to turn to.
But there's Anne, and on Sunday
you may find yourself on her couch watching
a guy you don't know make harassing
phone calls for an hour and a half. It'll be
warm and the diner across the street will be
closed and you won't ever want that hour
and a half to end—

maybe like the neighbors, the times they keep
their lights on all night, as if waiting
for something. Waiting for a son who never
existed to walk through their door at four AM,
tiptoe into their bedroom and whisper
quietly, I'm sorry, I'm sorry not only for arriving
late but for everything, all of the trouble
I've caused, all the heartache and pain, all
the nights of waiting up until morning
angry, or helpless, wanting to do something
but not knowing what. Maybe it's like
a New Year's gathering, eight people
at an oblong table, a toasting to eternal
life, a ninety-five dollar plate of lobster and a few
Italian language tapes, some drunkenness
and passing out while trying to figure out
who killed who in the conservatory.
Thankfully, there was no dancing, though
the wallet was recovered, a new species of animal
classified and an appetizer of oranges and olive
oil served upon someone's triumphant
return. Maybe it's like the time Felix
came over and said, I'm going back
to Buffalo but my heart will always be
in California and I just feel like
I'm writing the same thing over and over
again but before you can react phone
calls are made, lines crossed,
and you're listening to a woman whispering
how much she loves this man, and it's you
but it's not you, you know, like a faceless
Dave in a dream you have about someone
you wish you could love and someone else

you've always loved who refuses to love you.
But this woman loves this man so
much you just pretend for that moment
it's you and the words she uses like always
and tenderness are referring to you. You have
to admit that this kind of thing is what
leads to a pile of *Bon Appetit* magazines
outside your door, maybe like the time
you found yourself alone in Denver at 5:30
on a Tuesday morning with some new knowledge
of Nebraska, something that says all
airline disasters were worth it for the world
because the flight data recorder taught us
a lesson we'd never imagined, how the copilot
seemed like he'd crossed over to a place
of silence and wisteria where his mother now
dead fourteen years stood dressed in black
and where everything became aggressively lush
and though we heard him cry out
just before impact, it seemed
more an action of impulse rather than desperation
and now we'll all somehow know
how to feel just before that moment
our time comes, just before our minivans
overturn outside Des Moines—we won't
sit there confused but we'll be prepared
to cross the line in our life vests, lockets
safely tucked away, awaiting the collision.
Maybe it's like that, or maybe it's like
the time you waited all evening for the woman
you loved to show up and she never did—
you found yourself walking out onto a frozen
lake, never looking back into your empty

house. It was so cold, and the stars so
encompassing you thought there was no way
you could ever turn back, that you had nothing
to do but keep going, like the time standing
in line for the Beast, King's Island, Cincinnati,
Ohio, July 24, 1998—
you realized this may not last forever,
any of this, and before long you were right—
Sarah left you and someone you'd never know
was horribly wounded in a third world cockfighting
accident.

Here it is. Enclosed is a detailed report
outlining the reasons we should be together.
If you have any questions, please refer
to appendix A. If you have any questions
about appendix A, please refer
to appendix B. It's March but it's cold. My cat is,
most likely, pregnant, as you already know.
Right now, she's crying and just before
you arrived this afternoon the swans
crossed over to the other side of the lake.
Maybe that means something, I don't
know. Dan's from Hamtramck and a recovering
cocaine addict, but through it all, his mother
stayed by his side. Everyone has something,
something all at once disastrous and wonderful
from the past. Once, my father knocked over
a cabinet of knickknacks, my mother grabbed me
from bed late at night, threatening to move
to Alabama. Once, I fell in love
with a woman who didn't love me. As you'll
see, I've added an interesting words often

mispronounced section, though you probably
already know how to pronounce à la carte.
Fruit cup is to buttermilk biscuit as yellow
sky is to pain. Settee is to miniature
golf as laurel is to zenith S-band
antenna. However you look at it, dangling
on the edge of a cliff in a minivan is no way
to spend an afternoon. Confusion, a play
in seven sets, each set more
spectacular and elaborate than the last. You
know, seven years ago I didn't
know what to do but at least I knew
somebody with a convertible. Whatever
happened to that guy? One day last
summer, as I walked out of Bigfoot,
I was offered house speakers by two
mysterious dudes in a van and yet
at the same time felt vibrantly alive,
but the next day the heat had taken its toll
and I saw a movie with Peggy. During autumn
in Bloomington the leaves descend so quickly
you don't even have time to feel vibrantly
alive. Please note Section Four: Drunken
Spree. For some reason, I can't
get that May evening in Knoxville out
of my head. Somebody I'd never speak to again
was getting married. Sarah was there. We
slept on a motel room floor
together, but I was in love. Where
did you go, Sarah? I know you're there,
somewhere, each time I return to Bloomington.
Also note the lack of punctuation
in Section Six. That was intentional. I was trying

to evolve as a person. Fear God and fear
nothing else. Be sure, too, to check out
Plate One: somewhere between the mall
and New York City, because hey,
you could be living somewhere worse
than the midwest and there's nothing like hurling
an easy chair into a river, is there?
An ideal transfer. Now, the reasons
we should be together. Clear away
the veils. You have green eyes.
You watch me when I'm looking away.
You once walked into a local pharmacy
in Manchester to ask where the orchard was.
It was September. You tear receipts into thousands
of pieces. You've never been to Turkey. You
were with me the day last August
when I ran onto the beach and didn't want
to turn back and you fell asleep
on my shoulder as we drove home. You wanted
to kiss me across from a church in
Mexico during a thunderstorm. And when
I almost died in Iowa, even though
it was three in the morning, even though I
was alongside my best friend, even
though Townes Van Zandt was singing
on the radio, I was thinking of you for that one,
white second I believed my life was over.

photo by Jason Bredle

Jason Bredle received degrees in English and Spanish from Indiana University and an MFA from the University of Michigan. His chapbook, *A Twelve Step Guide*, was winner of the 2004 New Michigan Press chapbook contest. He lives in Chicago and works at a translation agency in Evanston, Illinois.

New Issues Poetry

Vito Aiuto, *Self-Portrait as Jerry Quarry*

James Armstrong, *Monument in a Summer Hat*

Claire Bateman, *Clumsy, Leap*

Kevin Boyle, *A Home for Wayward Girls*

Jason Bredle, *Standing in Line for the Beast*

Michael Burkard, *Pennsylvania Collection Agency*

Christopher Bursk, *Ovid at Fifteen*

Anthony Butts, *Fifth Season; Little Low Heaven*

Kevin Cantwell, *Something Black in the Green Part of Your Eye*

Gladys Cardiff, *A Bare Unpainted Table*

Kevin Clark, *In the Evening of No Warning*

Cynie Cory, *American Girl*

Peter Covino, *Cut Off the Ears of Winter*

James D'Agostino, *Nude with Anything*

Jim Daniels, *Night with Drive-By Shooting Stars*

Joseph Featherstone, *Brace's Cove*

Lisa Fishman, *The Deep Heart's Core Is a Suitcase*

Noah Eli Gordon, *A Fiddle Pulled from the Throat of a Sparrow*

Robert Grunst, *The Smallest Bird in North America*

Paul Guest, *The Resurrection of the Body and the Ruin of the World*

Robert Haight, *Emergences and Spinner Falls*

Mark Halperin, *Time as Distance*

Myronn Hardy, *Approaching the Center*

Brian Henry, *Graft*

Edward Haworth Hoeppner, *Rain Through High Windows*

Cynthia Hogue, *Flux*

Joan Houlihan, *The Mending Worm*

Christine Hume, *Alaskaphrenia*

Josie Kearns, *New Numbers*

David Keplinger, *The Clearing; The Prayers of Others*

Maurice Kilwein Guevara, *Autobiography of So-and-So: Poems in Prose*

Ruth Ellen Kocher, *When the Moon Knows You're Wandering;*
      One Girl Babylon

Gerry LaFemina, *Window Facing Winter*

Steve Langan, *Freezing*

Lance Larsen, *Erasable Walls*

David Dodd Lee, *Abrupt Rural; Downsides of Fish Culture*

M.L. Liebler, *The Moon a Box*

Alexander Long, *Vigil*

Deanne Lundin, *The Ginseng Hunter's Notebook*

Barbara Maloutas, *In a Combination of Practices*

Joy Manesiotis, *They Sing to Her Bones*

Sarah Mangold, *Household Mechanics*

Gail Martin, *The Hourglass Heart*

David Marlatt, *A Hog Slaughtering Woman*

Louise Mathias, *Lark Apprentice*

Gretchen Mattox, *Buddha Box; Goodnight Architecture*

Lydia Melvin, *South of Here*

Carrie McGath, *Small Murders*

Paula McLain, *Less of Her; Stumble, Gorgeous*

Sarah Messer, *Bandit Letters*

Wayne Miller, *Only the Senses Sleep*

Malena Mörling, *Ocean Avenue*

Julie Moulds, *The Woman with a Cubed Head*

Marsha de la O, *Black Hope*

C. Mikal Oness, *Water Becomes Bone*

Bradley Paul, *The Obvious*

Jennifer Perrine, *The Body Is No Machine*

Katie Peterson, *This One Tree*

Elizabeth Powell, *The Republic of Self*

Margaret Rabb, *Granite Dives*

Rebecca Reynolds, *Daughter of the Hangnail; The Bovine Two-Step*

Martha Rhodes, *Perfect Disappearance*

Beth Roberts, *Brief Moral History in Blue*

John Rybicki, *Traveling at High Speeds* (expanded second edition)

Mary Ann Samyn, *Inside the Yellow Dress, Purr*

Ever Saskya, *The Porch is a Journey Different From the House*

Mark Scott, *Tactile Values*

Hugh Seidman, *Somebody Stand Up and Sing*

Martha Serpas, *Côte Blanche*

Diane Seuss-Brakeman, *It Blows You Hollow*